WHEN YOU NEED

A Reminder of How Loved You Are

By Phoebe Garnsworthy

Dear Soul

Even though it feels like everything in my life is falling apart, I believe in you.
I believe in your divinity. I believe in your power.
I believe that you are supporting and guiding me forward.
I trust that the answers will come forth to me when the time is right, and for now, I will hold faith to keep walking forward and to keep standing strong.
I promise to surrender and believe.
I know that when I surrender, I will receive.
And so, I will release my fear of the unknown by believing that all is as it should be.
And if I find myself in doubt of your greatness, I will kneel upon the ground, place my hands upon the Earth, and surrender, surrender, and surrender while knowing the truth that all your blessings are already within me.
I will close my eyes and listen to your guidance without hesitation.
I will find my power within to persevere.
I will heal my energy with the nurturing vibrations of Source Energy.
I will surrender with faith into your love.

Also by Phoebe Garnsworthy
Daily Rituals: Positive Affirmations to Attract Love, Happiness, and Peace
I Affirm My Power
Align with Soul
Remember the Witch Within
Define Me Divine Me: a Poetic Display of Affection
and still, the Lotus Flower Blooms
Lost Nowhere: A Journey of Self-Discovery (Vol. 1)
Lost Now Here: The Road to Healing (Vol. 2)
The Spirit Guides: A Short Novella

www.PhoebeGarnsworthy.com

WHEN YOU NEED A REMINDER OF HOW LOVED YOU ARE
ISBN: 978-0-9954119-7-5
Paperback

Copyright © 2023 by Phoebe Garnsworthy
Cover Illustration by Mariana Dapi
Editing by Word Witch Copy Consulting, LLC.

All rights reserved. No part of this publication may be reproduced, distributed, or transmitted in any form or by any means, without prior written permission from the author.

Contents

Dear Soul	3
Introduction	8
How to Use This Book	10
The Choice	13
Today I Choose Peace	14
Today I Choose Calm	15
When You Need to Wake Up and Start Another Day	18
When You Need to Love Yourself More	20
When You Need to Trust the Divine Timing of Your Life	22
When You Need to Feel Supported	24
When You Need to Let Go of Negative Thoughts	26
When You Need to Heal	28
When You Need to Forgive	30
When You Need a Reminder to Keep Going	32
When You Need Confidence in Who You Are	34
When You Need to Heal from a Bad Breakup	36
When You Need to Control Your Emotions	38
When You Need a Break and Are Exhausted	40
When You Need to Have Faith That All is as it Should Be	42
When You Need to Find Your Life Purpose	44
When You Need Something to Change	46
When You Need the Courage to Find a New Job	48
When You Need More Self-Care	50
When You Need to Believe in Something	52
When You Need a Break From People	54
When You Need Self-Discipline	56
When You Need to Keep Going After Failure	58

When You Need to Live in the Present Moment	60
When You Need to Stop Feeling Lonely	62
When You Need to Remember How Incredible You Are	64
When You Need to Heal From Someone Who Hurt You	66
When You Need to Be Forgiven for Hurting Someone	68
When You Need to Remind Yourself of How Far You've Come	70
When You Need to Let Go of Fear	72
When You Need to Be Held	74
When You Need Life to Flow Differently	76
When You Need to Feel Healthy	78
When You Need to Believe in Yourself Because No One Else Is	80
When You Need to Let Go of the Past	82
When You Need to Heal From the Passing of a Loved One	84
When You need to Find More Joy and Happiness	86
When You Need a Sign	88
When You Need Freedom	90
When You Need to Find Calm Amidst the Chaos	92
When You Need Clarity Over Your Life	94
When You need to Go to Sleep After a Difficult Day	96
Today	99
About the Author	101
Other Books by Phoebe Garnsworthy	102

Introduction

Every now and again something rattles your belief in the Universe. Something breaks the confidence in yourself, and you lose the connection with your intuition. The voice of your soul fades, your resilience becomes weak, and you are crushed, unable to move forward. How do you pick yourself up? How do you keep going when everything seems so far from ever going again? You don't. You sit with it. You feel it. You enter that darkness and allow it to consume you. Cry, scream, shout. Let that energy move through you, and move it out. And when it's all gone, what's left? Emptiness. But inside that emptiness is energy. And energy never dies, it transforms. So the energy that you have released is being renewed, regenerated, and re-birthed. The question now is, how do you want that energy to be reborn?

You have more power at this moment because you are starting anew but with greater wisdom than before. You have more strength because, although what you went through was heartbreaking, you're still here, willing to learn, and that takes courage.

Your soul is singing love songs to you. Can you hear it? Listen deeply to what it is saying. Follow the voice of your intuition clearly. You are being told what to do and how to keep going.

The answers are within you, reminding you how to breathe amidst the smoke and teaching you how to swim through the chaos.

And most importantly, the voice of your soul is bringing you home. Back to the truth of where it is that you come from. Back to the safe space of harmonizing vibrations and connection as one with Source Energy. Retreat back to this divine essence and heed the wisdom waiting for you here. Nurture love through your body, heal your mind, and return to reality with confidence, resilience, and grace as you embrace the ever-changing rhythm of life's challenges.

Welcome to the greatest transformation you have ever asked for. Today you will find your flow. Today you will surrender unto the magical workings of the Universe. Today you will live with ease and trust. You will surrender into the unknown willingly, with a deep, profound knowing that the Universe is looking after you. You don't have to hold onto this pain, fear, or worry any longer, for you will feel and believe in your divinity. Allow yourself to be held in the infinite space of unconditional love and boundless possibilities. Today you will understand that everything happening to you has always been happening for you. And you will see this so clearly with your new change of perspective. You will accept the way your life is flowing and embody the belief that everything is right on time. And you will find peace. And you will feel loved as you surrender wholeheartedly to the magical workings of the Universe.

How to Use This Book

This little book is your source of solace. It will provide you with motivation and inspiration for any time of day that you're feeling troubled. Think of it as your reminder to reconnect to the wisdom within you. It will help provide you with the clarity and emotional support you need to overcome any challenges in your day. Each page is woven with spiritual philosophy to soothe and nurture your soul as you remember the innate wisdom embedded deep in your heart.

Bring yourself into the present moment, and allow your perception of what is to realign with the profound understanding that you hold the key to your ultimate transformation. Find peace in this knowing, as you remember that you are divinely guided with love—always—and that, therefore, everything is going to be okay.

You can open this book at random, or you can peruse the table of contents and find the theme that resonates with your current struggles. Each chapter will provide you with words of comfort, support, and love to help you navigate through this difficult time.

The wisdom in your chosen chapter will ignite the voice of your intuition to tell you the truth about what you need to know. This wisdom is merely the inspiration—an invitation—to listen to your soul. For your soul is the greatest healer you could ever ask for.

And only when we learn how to trust and listen to that voice of our soul, will we find the confidence and courage to persevere and continue on our life path with resilience and strength.

Have a journal and pen ready to write down any thoughts that come through to you after you read the message. Any fears, stress, or worries that are holding you back from stepping forward into greatness will be given an opportunity to heal and release. But remember that it is up to you to do the healing, it is up to you to let it go.

Allow any words, thoughts, or emotions to rise to the surface. Challenge those thoughts and find the truth of what they are trying to tell you. Heed their wisdom and apply it to your life to find the peace you are seeking. All that you will need is a willingness and commitment to yourself to make those changes.

And when you feel ready, transform that energy. Release, renew, and rebirth your perception of what lies before you. You have the power and ability to change your thoughts by simply choosing to shift your perception. And the way to do this is by listening to your soul and being open to the invitation. And that invitation is ready for you, waiting to be discovered within these pages. So take a deep breath, turn the page, and let me share with you what you need to know today.

The Choice

I know life has been challenging, but it was necessary to steer you on the right path, to help you understand the strength of your own resilience. You have the power to accomplish anything that you want, to live the life that you desire. But to get to this place of manifested consciousness, the Universe may test you along the way. It may push you to see if it's what you truly want. And if you persevere and stay aligned with your true self, then all will be well. Even if you waiver along the pathway longer than you think you should, don't be too hard on yourself. Because whatever is meant to be will be waiting for you. Whatever is meant for you is coming. Regardless of your actions, your beliefs, or your doing.

But if you do choose to play a part in your destiny, you will reap the sweetest rewards in ways you couldn't possibly imagine. For you will be co-creating your life with the Universe. And when you conjoin with the miraculous wonders around you, you will create the most incredible life that you have always desired.

The choice is yours.

Today I Choose Peace

*I choose to feel the harmonious vibrations
that echo within my soul.
I choose to seek refuge in the peaceful energy
that soothes my being.
At any point, I know I can relax my mind by breathing
this gentle energy that flows within me and around me.
And if I somehow forget this truth,
I will simply close my eyes and bring myself back home.*

Today I Choose Calm

*I choose to bring my attention to the present moment.
I choose to align with the powers of my Higher Self.
I choose to be one with the vibrations of the Universe.
And if at any point I forget this simple truth,
I will call upon the blissful energy of my soul,
and I will find my way back home.*

When You Need

A Reminder of How Loved You Are

When You Need to Wake Up and Start Another Day

Hello, beautiful shining star.

Yes, I'm talking to you.
You, with that energy radiating so brilliantly.
You, who cares for everyone so deeply.
You, who has endured hardships but has never stopped smiling.

Yes, you.
Today is your day.

Today you will receive all the success that you have been craving. Today you will live freely without regret, without any pain or hurt in your mind. Today you will let go of the past and feel excited for the future. Today you will step into the true, beautiful version of yourself that you really are. Today you will stop hiding your gifts. Today you will stop apologizing for your talents and intelligence.

Today you will love wholeheartedly, starting with yourself. Today you will live as the divine light-being that you are, with radiant love overflowing from within you. Because you deserve the best. You have always been giving your love lavishly, and you will finally receive all that love in return.

Today you will let go of any negativity, fear, or stress. It will simply melt away as you breathe with ease. Because you are choosing to align with the truth of your soul. And your soul holds no space for negativity. Your soul is pure peace and calmly collected.

Today great change and transformation will take place. Because you are blessed. You are blissful. And today you will step forward with confidence in your stride.

Today your greatest desires and dreams will manifest with ease. Today you will feel healthy. Today you will love your body. Today you will honor your body with the respect it deserves. Today you will make your ancestors proud. Today you will hear your angels and loved ones cheering you on.

Today is your day. But this day is just like every other day. For it is what you make of it. But now you finally realize that there is nothing holding you back from receiving your dreams except for yourself, and so, today is the day that you will focus on creating the life that you have been dreaming of. Because today you believe in your power, in your unlimited existence, in your ability to manifest your greatest desires. Yes, beautiful soul, today is your day.

When You Need to Love Yourself More

You have an abundance of loving energy flowing within you. This energy radiates with pure bliss and peaceful vibrations without you even trying. You have the ability to be confident, resilient, brave, and talented. So why aren't you believing in your divine presence in this world?

You were born into this life for a reason. You were created on this Earth to receive incredible experiences. You are always connected to the divine creation of the Universe. You are an extension of its love. If you think too long about it, you may feel dwarfed in your true greatness. But to allow that fear to consume you is to create a limiting belief, and you are so much better than that. So today let that fear go. Peel away the layers of hurt, pain, or sadness that are holding you back from living as your true self. Let go of all the negative thoughts, limiting beliefs, and past regret, because these thoughts are serving you no more. Break free from the grief in your heart, and forgive yourself for any time that you were less than kind. Remember your power and life purpose.

You were born for a reason. And that reason is to be your authentic self, to love your life, and to share your authenticity with the world. Don't you want to see what incredible vibrations you can create in this life? Don't you want to live with truth in your stance and praise in your heart? The pathway to embody all of this is to love and honor yourself. I don't mean to just love your body and your face. I mean love your soul.

Love the essence of who you are. Love the divine light-being inside of what makes you, you.

To love your soul, you need to honor, listen, and connect with it. And you can do this very easily by discovering what brings you the most joy in this world. Where does your soul thrive? What do you love about yourself that makes you, you? Write a small paragraph about yourself starting with *I am*. List only words that radiate positive and beautiful vibrations, because that's what you are. Read those words and repeat them to yourself in the mirror every day until you start believing in them.

You are beautiful. You are divine. You are blessed. You have so much good in your heart, I can feel it. I know that you do too. You care about self-improvement and strive to always do better, and that is the key to withstanding unwanted change. For you will experience many highs and lows in this life that will force you to adapt and transform. So face those changes with wisdom, and act with grace. And let that beautiful light within you expand and blossom. Take care of your mind, body, and soul, and in return, you will lead a deeply rewarding and fulfilling life. This is your destiny—to live a life that you love. And it all starts with loving yourself, taking care of yourself, and listening to the voice of your soul. You have the tools within you to learn how to love yourself, so take the time to get to know yourself, and practice that self-love consistently every day.

When You Need to Trust the Divine Timing of Your Life

I understand your frustration and feel your pain. You can want something so badly, and put all your energy into making it happen, but sometimes it's just not enough. And there comes a moment when you need to surrender and trust that it will happen when it is meant to. The thing is, the Universe doesn't work on the same timeline as us here on Earth. The Universe has its own divine timing that has nothing to do with hours or days, but to do with our spiritual growth. We will receive our rewards or hardships regardless of our meddling because the timing of these things isn't up to us, it's up to our soul contract. So what do we do? How do we keep going when it feels like nothing makes sense and we are losing the fight? We just *keep going*. We trust, we believe, and we surrender to what is.

Everything that you crave in your life is going to be delivered to you. Do not stress about that. Do not worry that you won't be given all that you desire. Because you will receive your dreams, and so much more. You will be gifted all the success that you crave. You will receive the faithful, deep love that you deserve. You will live the life that you want because you believe that it is the life that you are meant to be living. So keep thinking that way. Keep believing and knowing that it will happen, and keep working hard to achieve the life that you want. Don't ever give up. Don't focus your energy elsewhere.

Keep supporting the growth of yourself, and keep the pathway open for the Universe to deliver its promises.

So often we want to run away and hide. So often we think that we are being handed cards that are unfair or a life that isn't fruitful. But your life is filled with pure love and healing vibrations with a great depth of emotion. Sometimes that emotion is dark and heavy, and other times it's light and blissful. Both of them deserve your acknowledgement and gratitude. Sometimes to receive our desired manifestations we need to endure hardships. We may be thrown down to the ground to prove that it's what we really want. Every time that you feel ready to let go of your goals, ask yourself, "Is this what my soul is craving?" And if it is, you will receive that blessing in due time. But remember, not on your time, on the Universe's time. And that time is the divine time. And that time, we don't know. All we know is that we need to surrender to what is, have faith in what will be, and trust that there is a divine power looking after us. Because there is. There always is. You are divinely guided and looked after by your angels, your spirit guides, and your ancestors. You are supported by the entire Universe. And every energy in this Universe wants you to receive your blessings. So don't give up now. Know that your time is coming. Keep going forward. One step forward. The next step forward. Again and again and again.

When You Need to Feel Supported

Today I journeyed to the unseen realms for you. I saw your Higher Self, standing strong, in the cosmos, looking over your life here on Earth. You were sending love to yourself, back to Earth, from far above. There was a love song singing from the voices of the Universe. And a message from your angels, telling you that they are watching over you. They are right next to you when you are crying. They are holding your hand when you are asking for help. They are watching over you while you sleep, sending you healing prayers and soothing vibrations. They are letting you know that all is okay, and that very soon, you will stand stronger than you ever have before. And most importantly, they want you to know that you are loved. You are so loved. So please, don't give up now.

Never fret, darling love. For you are divinely supported by grace. Do not fear, darling child, for you are forever held by the love of the Universe. Do not worry about a thing, because the angels of your ancestors are embracing your soul. They are in the unseen realms holding you tightly with love. They are in the cosmic world wishing you well and letting you know that everything is okay.

You are surrounded by an abundance of love and support at every moment of every day. There is nothing for you to worry about, because they have never forgotten about you. You have never been left alone for one second. Your soul is loved. Your body is beautiful. Your mind is intelligent.

And everything that is happening to you right now is meant to happen. Everything that you are going through has the ability to make you more resilient, more courageous, and more powerful. It is all happening as it is meant to. So whatever you are feeling, whatever you are going through, just know that it won't last forever. You will move through it, you will smile again, laugh, and love, and be happy in life once more. And this pain that you now feel will be a distant memory. For it will have transformed into great wisdom. You will have channeled your wound into your power and carry it like a medal of triumph.

You are strong and capable of handling anything that comes your way. And if you forget the power of your soul, ask your angels, ask your spirit guides and ancestors to send you the support that you crave. Close your eyes and call out to their beauty. Feel their angelic vibrations of peace and harmony dance upon your skin. Open your heart to feel the nurturing love of their endless blessings embracing your soul. You are never alone. You are forever loved, guided, and honored by the divine, beating heart of the Universe. Remember this whenever you imagine yourself to be lonely. And don't be shy to ask for help, to ask for guidance or support from another. When you feel ready, open your heart to receive the signs from Spirit all around you. Request your blessings from the angels above, and let them hold you in a sweet embrace of luminous, loving light energy.

When You Need to Let Go of Negative Thoughts

The time has come for you to let go of those thoughts and be at peace with your mind. Those negative thoughts will never help you. They are weighing you down and holding you back from allowing yourself to shine as the radiant, divine light that you are.

You have so much love within you. And this love in your heart beats in harmony with the vibrations of the Universe. You encompass all the talents, intelligence, and possibilities to attain the success that you desire, but you can't receive your destiny while holding onto these negative vibrations. You cannot step into your greatest self until you let go of those dark and heavy thoughts. You cannot be free to live as your authentic self while you are focusing on any energy that is keeping you small.

You are destined for greatness. You have the ability to create any life that you want, and you can be anyone that you wish to be. You have so much potential, so many talents, and endless possibilities around you that can raise you up high. But you are holding yourself back because you keep choosing to listen to limiting beliefs. And you are stopping yourself from succeeding because you are focusing your attention on the past. It's because you are choosing to align with pain, when really, you need to live in alignment with love. And you have so much love within you. You have so much love around you.

You are an abundance of loving-light energy that is always surrounded with healing love from Source Creation.

So today choose to let go of those painful thoughts and limiting beliefs. Choose to release them. Face them head-on, and feel them. Accept them, but know that they don't belong to you. Know that you can choose to let them go. Use your breath, use your body, use your mind to release and renew that energy within you. Dance, scream, shout, sing, do anything that moves that energy from your mind and opens the space for new vibrations to take their place. Remember your power to create your destiny. Remember your ability to transmute energy. Remember your strength to gravitate toward high vibrations. And remember your power to choose your thoughts.

Today choose thoughts that lift you up higher. Choose thoughts that support your greater good. Choose thoughts that align with the deep inner yearnings of your soul that nurture your vibration, that feed you love and harmonize your energy. Choose thoughts that make you feel good, make you feel healthy, and inspire spiritual growth. Choose to align with the best version of yourself possible, and find the thoughts that support that version of you. And any thought that doesn't unify with this wonderful manifestation of who you are and the life you wish to lead, simply let them go and pick up something new to invite into its place.

When You Need to Heal

Whatever you are going through right now, I want you to know that you are not alone. Your angels, your ancestors, and your spirit guides are close by, supporting you as you navigate this process of healing. They are sending you an abundance of nurturing energy and holding you with the hand of divinity. Feel yourself cocooned in this love, and open your heart to receive those healing vibrations.

I hold great faith that you will let go of the past and find the strength to heal. I have no doubt in my mind that it's going to happen. You are going to heal and feel more confident than you have ever felt before. And when you finally move through this pain, you will receive an abundance of divine energy and wisdom from this experience. You have the desire to attract this wisdom and move through this pain, so it's only a matter of time before it comes to fruition. Hold that faith close to your heart, and enter this exploration of transformation with curiosity, lightness, and patience. Face the experience with an open mind, and trust the process. Trust the pain. Trust the emotions. Trust that this is where you need to be. Confront the emotions and feel them, truly feel them. Then let yourself be free of them.

You have so many nurturing resources around you to help you heal. Mother Nature is your greatest loving support. She will hold you tightly, she will send you love and take away your pain. She will gift you lightness, love, and peace, and she wants nothing in return but to be felt, seen, and heard. So go outside and speak with her.

Explore the lands around you to connect with her. Just be with her, in silence, in her womb of creation—with an open heart—and feel the vibrations of her nurturing love resonate profoundly within you.

Know that all will be revealed at the right time. But until it does, do whatever you can to make yourself feel better. See people, or don't see people. Curl up with a good book, or have a glass (or three) of your favorite drink. Indulge in massages and self-love practices. Decorate your life with the beautiful energy you deserve. Keep moving the core of your soul toward the vibrations that lift you up high. Because when you do, your soul will start to thrive, you will begin to dance, and you will find yourself singing a new tune. One that aligns with the pathway of peace. One that brings forth beautiful thoughts, connections, and laughter. And then one day, very soon, you won't even realize, but you will have healed. You will have become stronger than you ever thought possible. You will feel confident, with a deep sense of support from the Universe. And you will have created a new perception of this experience along with an unshakable bond of knowing that everything happened as it was meant to. And that everything is right on time.

When You Need to Forgive

The time has come for you to make peace with your past. If you have learned all you can from this experience, and it no longer serves your ability to grow, then it's time to forgive, release, and let go. If it has played its role, and you have learned the lesson, your perception of the world has transformed from this experience, and your compassion for yourself and others has deepened. So now is the time to let the experience go—to forgive and forget. You have the ability to be an alchemist of energy. You can allow the past to simply wash through you, and you can transmute it into wisdom, into greatness. And you can move on with your life and live the great success story that you are meant to live.

But this life of peace and glory cannot happen if you are still holding on to this past pain. You cannot evolve if you are constantly looking back and wishing for something to be different. And you cannot be your greatest self if you are always placing the blame on others for something going wrong in your life. So today let all that blame go. Discover the compassion in your heart to forgive another, with the same depth and love you offer yourself. Enter the pain boldly, and listen to its wisdom, learn from this experience, and make a choice to forgive.

Today is the day for forgiveness. Know that they didn't know any better at the time. Know that you were doing the best you knew how to. Know that with time everything heals, but in order for complete healing to take place, forgiveness needs to happen. Accept your past.

Accept your pain. Accept your emotions, and let go of guilt or shame for feeling these emotions. You are entitled to your emotions. Own that space. Own how you feel, and let it be a part of you. Speak your truth. Create your boundaries. Learn from this lesson. And then, when you are ready, let that energy completely wash through you. Let your past be a part of your life, but don't let it rule your life. Let it be a chapter in your story, but not the whole story. You have many more chapters to live. You have so much more life to experience. And that is a great thing. This is just a small piece of your journey that will provide you with the tools to transform into greatness. And you will encounter many more tools along your life journey.

So today, let the energy of the past move through you. Feel the emotions with honest intentions as you choose to release them in a healthy way. And find the peace within your heart that chooses to forgive. Holding onto anger or pain will hold you back from transforming. Holding tightly to your grief does not help you to see things clearly. Holding firmly to your story does not allow new stories to take place. Let it go. Open yourself to healing. Open yourself to forgiveness.

I forgive you. I forgive myself. I choose peace. I choose to let go. I choose to heal. I choose for a new story to light my pathway. I choose to transform into greatness.

When You Need a Reminder to Keep Going

Trust me when I tell you that everything is going to work out just fine. Actually, it's going to work out even better than fine. Your life is going to be greater than anything you could ever imagine. How do I know? Because you are destined for incredible things! You are destined to receive all the love, success, and laughter that you crave. You will heal. You will live a long and happy life in good health, surrounded by your loved ones. You will triumph over defeat. You will get through this pain. You will become the person you've been dreaming about. You will. I promise.

I know this for a fact, because this is what you want. And you will receive anything and everything that you want because, deep down, your heart is pure. Your love is overflowing. Your kindness is nurturing. And you have a beautiful light shining from within your soul. That shining light is lighting up the whole world. The whole Universe can see it. The whole Universe can feel it. And that light is attracting angels and your ancestors to give you strength to help you carry on. All you need to do is ask them for their blessings. They are waiting for you to call out to them. They are waiting for you to ask for their help. And they will be there. They have never left you. They have always been with you. They are always guiding you. They are always supporting you and sending you love from afar. Lean into their love. Pray to them. Give thanks to them. And be at peace in knowing this truth.

You have been walking along a dark pathway, but there is a golden light at the end of the tunnel. And that golden light is you. You are the answer to moving through this. You are the solution to your life's problems. You hold the blessings that you crave. Close your eyes and feel the power of your soul guiding you. Search within to find the answers. Search within to find your peace and strength. It's there. It's waiting for you to call out to it, harness it, and take hold of it.

You will get through this pain. You will move through this struggle. You will succeed and step into greatness. You are an incredibly gifted, beautiful soul with endless talents. Everything that you want is coming. Everything that you need is right on time. Be patient with the divine timing of Source Creation. Close your eyes, take a deep breath, and feel the love of your soul as you embody the Universe's divine presence. And stay here in this sacred space of nirvana, until you find the calm that you deserve.

Remember, you are divinely supported. You are always on your pathway toward your ultimate destiny. You will receive everything that your soul is craving. You will laugh and love and be happy again. You will. I promise you, you will.

When You Need Confidence in Who You Are

The only person holding you back from stepping into your power is you. You are incredible, talented, beautiful, and worthy of living your best life, so why aren't you doing it? What is it that is stopping you from believing in your worth? When we lack confidence in ourselves, what it really means is that we lack love for ourselves. And the only reason we don't love ourselves enough is because we don't truly comprehend the strength of our unique talents.

The confidence you seek is buried deep within your heart. It is shining brightly from your soul, waiting for you to acknowledge its truth. Every day, make an effort to step closer to this space. Make a commitment to grow your confidence by implementing self-love and self-care practices into your daily life. Sprinkle love notes to your mind through words of affirmation and meditation practices. Become best friends with your soul by accepting yourself as you are in this moment. Remember your worth, remember your ability to create the life that you desire. Call out to your soul and ask to feel its innate beauty. Then open your heart to receive these blessings.

You have so many strengths already within you. It's time to acknowledge them with gratitude as you strive to improve the areas of your life that you wish to be better. Every day, do something where your true self thrives, for that action will continue to build confidence within you. Find the spiritual tools that support your personal and spiritual development. Self-reflect with curiosity over your past actions. Practice self-awareness with ease.

Strengthen your inner power through exploration, education, and experience. Try something new each day and see how incredible and versatile you really are. The more you practice being true to yourself in new environments, the greater your confidence will grow. And the braver, more courageous, and more caring you will be to yourself and others.

You have endured great challenges through your past lives, and that wisdom of your innate ability has carried over into your life today. This alone gives you the confidence to be true to yourself. But you also walk carrying the knowledge and skills of your ancestors. Each one of them made it possible for you to be standing here right now. And their strength lives on within you. Talk to your loved ones who have passed, and ask for memories of your past lives to be shown to you. Ask the Universe to send you the wisdom that you seek. And open your heart to receive whatever comes your way. Believe in the power of your existence. Believe in the uniqueness of your presence. Believe in how incredibly beautiful, talented, intelligent, and gifted you are. You are alive, and for this reason, you are meant to be living here. Take charge of your life by harnessing your inner power and continue to adapt, continue to grow, and continue to breed joy and love within yourself with every breath and every step forward.

When You Need to Heal from a Bad Breakup

When we reflect on our past relationships, we often remember them better than they actually were. We idolize them, forgetting the bad and only remembering the good. And because of the way our brain works, the more often we remember memories to be better than they were, the more real those false memories become, and pretty soon, we start to believe our own lies as the truth.

How honest are you being with yourself about this past relationship that didn't work out? How right was this "perfect someone" for you, really? The moment we let go of what we think we had and learn to accept our reality for what it is, the sooner our healing will commence. And once we are healed, we can look back on our past relationships as a great life lesson.

Every doorway closed holds the power to a new beginning. And every new beginning is a wonderful opportunity to deepen the connection with your soul. But in order to embrace this new love for yourself, you need to let go. Because you can't keep holding onto what was. You can't keep holding onto fake memories or imaginary projections of how good you think it could be. The moment you let go of this attachment is when the true, infinite power will come to you.

Falling in love with the wrong person doesn't mean you've wasted your time. There's no way you could've known that it wasn't going to work out. And even though it didn't work out, you grew, you evolved, and you learned a valuable life lesson. Hold comfort in knowing that. Remind yourself that you did the best you could to make that relationship work. You acted according to your level of awareness at the time, so be at peace with your actions, words, and decisions. If you are uneasy with your past, forgive yourself. Forgive the other person for not knowing better at the time. Know that both of you acted according to your level of awareness, your level of consciousness, and your level of wisdom. You need to forgive yourself. This lesson brings an invitation to be clear with your boundaries and desires for your relationships moving forward. This lesson reminds you to prioritize your needs and wants and lets you know that your perfect someone will honor and respect those wishes too.

You know, deep within, that the right person will never disrespect you or make you feel insecure about your worth. You know that the right person will never let you go, or choose another as your replacement. You know that the right person will love you for who you are, wholeheartedly, and that you will reciprocate this love with equal depth and intensity. And the right person is coming to you. Don't worry. Don't stress. You don't need to go searching. Just focus on healing and being the best version of yourself by pouring self-love into your heart. Pursue your goals, and have faith that your soulmate will arrive when the time is right.

When You Need to Control Your Emotions

Emotions are vibrations that are created from your energy. Although they may feel so potent and powerful, it doesn't mean that they are the absolute truth. It doesn't mean that you always need to react. Rather, your emotions are trying to communicate with you; they want to show you something. Your emotions have a message for you, and the best way to bring harmony to your emotions is by listening to what they have to say. Every message holds an opportunity for transformation. And this transformation will bring you self-awareness and a change of perception. Your emotions can provide you with profound wisdom if you choose to enter them gracefully with ease.

Sit with your emotions. Let them vibrate within you. Ask them what they need and how you can best serve them. Journal through the feelings that arise within you, and reflect upon them. Ask them why they are stirring within you, and analyze them. Then when you feel ready, choose to allow the energy to move through you. Do this by combining meditation and the force of your breath to release these stuck emotions, and absorb new vibrations. Use visualization, and amplify your experience. Truly release those emotions stuck within you. And then finally, have a good night's sleep. Let your emotions have their chance to exit your body and mind. The next day, see how you feel. Is the emotion still arising? What does it need in order to be heard and released?

If there is an action you can take to support its need, now you can do so. For you have had time to reevaluate the situation with a different perspective. Act or speak according to your divine truth, from a place of love, and let your emotions have their say. Choose your words wisely as you communicate your truth. Connect with your emotions often to create a life that supports the ultimate version of yourself.

You have the power to control any emotion. You have the ability to transform your energy into whatever vibration you choose. The more you participate in spiritual practices such as meditation, grounding to the Earth, and having a mindful awareness of the present moment, the easier it will be for you to transform your energy. Use your breath to release your emotions to the cosmos. Use your intention to feed your emotions to the Earth. And then open your heart to receive new vibrations, new energy, new love, and new peace. You are an alchemist of energy, and you can transmute those vibrations within however you wish to. Use your intention and your actions to transform yourself and your energy into greatness. You are being gifted with an abundance of power and loving-light energy. Believe in your ability to recreate, realign, and replenish yourself. There is so much power within you. Step into this power bravely, and release your energy with confidence.

When You Need a Break and Are Exhausted

I see you, light warrior. You have been moving so fast and working so hard, and you're tired. You are scared to stop because this motivation for success is what keeps you alive and keeps your life flowing. But your current lifestyle is not sustainable, and if you do not choose to slow down on your own, you will be forced to, in some way or another. Your soul is pleading for a moment of rest. Your soul is asking for a moment of peace. You have been chasing the dream for far too long. You need calm. You need tranquility. You need heart-nurturing vibrations. You need time to honor yourself. Your soul is demanding that you gift yourself time. Why aren't you giving yourself this rest? You deserve it. You are worthy of it. And you need it. Because when we feed love to ourselves, we renew our energy to be stronger than ever before. When we prioritize ourselves, we can provide an abundance of love to gift others in return. And when we choose to look after our health as a priority, we have more energy to work more efficiently and confidently toward our life goals.

Listen to your soul. What is it saying today? What kind of environment is it craving? Where can you find the peace that you need? Your soul is telling you the answer. But you might be too scared to listen. But don't ignore that voice. Because wherever it is that your soul is craving is where you need to go. But perhaps the place you need to go is impossible right now. Maybe it's far away, or maybe you don't know how to get there. Or maybe you are too stressed for time; that to leave everything for a moment is simply not an option. That's okay.

All we need to do is find peace together here in the present moment. And the energy to soothe you is right at your fingertips. Those vibrations will heal you within a second of its presence. Simply close your eyes, place your hand on your heart, and feel the energy of your soul.

Focus on the divine, vibrating presence of your beautiful soul. Listen to it. What is it saying? Does it say you need peace? Journey deep within, and sit in meditation as you feel the resounding pleasure of your soul's divinity caressing you with nurturing softness. Do you need love? Give yourself love, go to the mirror, and tell yourself all the beautiful things about yourself. Speak positive affirmations that focus on your strengths and talents. Do you need happiness? Give yourself happiness by choosing to align with high vibrations. Create your life to be filled with all the wondrous blessings that you deserve. Because you *do* deserve them. Because you *can* find them. Because your soul is telling you the way forward, the way to achieve them.

Take a deep breath in and out, and calm yourself with your own energy. If you find resistance within your energy, keep moving through that space with deep breaths, words of love, and intention for peace. Take another deep breath. Rest your hand on your heart. Take another deep breath, and remember the divine beauty of your eternal light within.

When You Need to Have Faith That All is as it Should Be

Everything in your life is always happening for a reason. It's a bigger reason than any of us can understand right now, but all we can do is trust and believe that the answers will come through when the time is right. Until that time comes, take a deep breath, and hold that faith tightly in your heart. Feel the weight of its power as you let go of how you think your life should be, and surrender to the unknown with trust and patience.

Before you entered this life, your soul chose a series of life lessons that would enable profound growth and wisdom. That wisdom you are to learn here will provide you with an incredible awareness of yourself, and your soul, and an understanding of life in relation to the entire cosmic Universe. You cannot get to this place by chance, you need to persevere through difficult times. You need to overcome challenges, and you will overcome challenges because your soul didn't choose things that you couldn't succeed at. Sometimes success is not always the definition of what you think it should be. For there is a greater master here at play. There is a specific vantage point of wisdom that can be impossible to comprehend; it can only be felt in order to be known. And that is what this challenge is for you. It provides you with the tools to step into greatness. It provides you with the ability to comprehend life in new ways. It is gifting you a new pathway to strengthen your connection with your soul and its unbreakable tie with the Universe.

Every challenge pushes us to either run away or come back to our soul and trust and believe in the magic of the unknown. Every challenge asks you for faith as it pushes you to your limits in order to receive your blessings. Don't fear the unknown. For you are always protected and supported by the Universe. You are always divinely guided by your soul, by your ancestors and spirit guides. Lean closer to that connection. Lean deeper into the love of yourself. And have faith that all will be revealed in the divine time.

Today, turn your awareness inward to your inner power. Turn your faith inward to feel the strength of your soul guiding you forward. And never lose hope. If you have lost it, take your time to find it again. Seek outside the normalities of your daily life, and find that glimmer of light that exists around you. It's there to be found. Sometimes we need to dig a little deeper and search in places we wouldn't normally go. But it's there. And your soul knows the pathway forward. So listen to its wisdom. Your strength to persevere through these times of darkness is already within you, holding you tightly and guiding you forward. It's there, deep within your heart; that feeling of love and never-ending support. Be gentle, be calm, and never forget that all is as it should be. All will be well. Find the faith inside of you that is telling you to keep going, and listen to it, trust it, and believe it as you surrender wholeheartedly into the now.

When You Need to Find Your Life Purpose

You are so talented, intelligent, and blessed. You hold a unique gift that no one else has. Your life purpose is to find that gift and to share it with the world. But how do we find it? How do we learn what is unlearnable? Because your gift comes naturally to you. It's a talent that you have been practicing for many lifetimes. It is your birthright. You don't need to be told how to do it, because you already know how. You just need to have the confidence to actually follow through and use it. And the more you practice using your talent and living your truth, the easier your life will flow.

We learn about our gifts and talents by listening to the voice of our soul and by moving our vibration closer to what brings us joy. Your soul is always telling you what you are good at through energy. It brings forth high vibrations when you do what it thrives at, and it brings you down low when you act out of alignment with who you really are.

Move closer to the things that light up your soul. Experiment and play with your truth. Try out new ideas and take risks. Reveal the areas in your life that bring you fulfillment, and do them more often. Find the right people in your life who bring you happiness, and spend time with them more. Communicate with your soul, and ask questions that prompt inspiration. Questions such as, what am I interested in? What comes naturally to me? If I could do anything in the world, what would it be? What activities do I enjoy the most? How can I apply my best qualities to my life work?

And when you ask your soul for guidance, trust the answers of your intuition. Be open to receiving signs from the spirit world. You are always guided, looked after, and nurtured from the unseen realms. You just need to keep walking forward and listening. You just need to keep moving your energy to experiment with new ideas and remember to trust yourself. Keep trying, keep exploring, and keep believing that your pathway will be illuminated very soon when the time is right.

You will find your life purpose. You will discover the pathway of your Higher Self. You will live a fulfilled life. Because you want it. And everything that you want, you will receive. But in order to receive, you need to be willing to learn. You need to be open-minded and curious to change and try out new things. You need to let go of fear and believe in your power and ability to walk your truth with greatness. You need to be patient and practice. Your destiny will not rush forward until you are ready to receive it. Your destiny will not expire, it will not fail to come to fruition. You have not lost time. You are right on time. Your destiny is here. Your life purpose is waiting and ready for you to take it. The question is, are you ready?

When You Need Something to Change

If you feel like you are standing still in your life, it's because you need to make a change. You have the power of creation within you, and your soul wants you to activate that power. Your soul wants you to do something that you have never done before. And that change is something that you have felt a calling for from within for a long time. But as you've grown older, you've begun to doubt yourself, and you've learned how to silence that voice. Perhaps, over time, you have lost confidence and faith as to whether you could succeed if you were to even try. Perhaps, with time, you have grown too bitter and weak to attempt something new. But today, you are held back no longer. For today a fire has ignited within you, pushing you forward with motivation and telling you to take charge.

When you finally take that leap of faith, you will realize that this is how your life has always been meant to be lived. You will feel liberated and aligned with your life's purpose, and everything in your life will finally make sense. When this happens, you may hold regret for not doing it sooner. But be patient with yourself. For you haven't lost time; you are right where you need to be. You are now ready to embark upon a great adventure of transformation! When you act upon your soul's wishes, the pathway laid out before you will become ever so clear, and you will realize that it has always been this way. So take that first step forward, and let the Universe support you in ways you never thought imaginable!

But if today you have no idea what change you are seeking, just recognizing that in itself is a great lesson to have learned. In order to know what we want, we need to know what we don't want. And often knowing what you don't want is the pathway to finding what you do. So try things out, and experiment. Push yourself to do something you've never done before. It could be something tiny that may seem insignificant, but its action is still building courage in your mind, its movement is still building your strength to leap—wild and free—when the opportunity of change presents itself to you. But if you still cannot find what it is that you're searching for, or what change you wish to embark upon, spend some time on your own, spend some time all alone, and listen to your soul. Connect with the voice of your intuition, and let it provide you with the answers that you seek. Let your soul feed you the wisdom you crave. Let your soul take control of your life as it moves its vibrations closer to the love and light of pure joy that it seeks. And then, my beauty, you will find your life to be decorated with all the trimmings of high vibrations and rewarding experiences that you crave. And this, to live with pure love and joy in itself, is all we need in life.

When You Need the Courage to Find a New Job

The way you have been spending your time isn't serving you anymore. It isn't giving you the opportunity to grow into the best version of yourself that you deserve to be living. It hasn't been providing you with the deep sense of fulfillment you have been craving. You know this, but right now your ego is bruised. You feel like you've failed if you were to give up and start something new. But hidden within that failure holds the most wonderful opportunity for transformation. And right now, you are about to embark upon the greatest transformation of your soul's wishes!

This change of career may come to you faster than expected, and perhaps it has already knocked upon your door, and you are hesitant to move forward. But do not fear what is behind that unknown door of mystery. Because behind that door is an opportunity to discover the real you, the incredible you, the version of yourself you have dreamed about becoming since you were a little child. That version of yourself is ready and waiting for you. But to step into your truth, your soul needs to close doors in other areas of your life. It had to be done so that you could embrace and live the life you desire. And now that you have, you have been gifted the chance to discover who it is you really are. Now is the moment you have been dreaming about all of your life. Now you can find the answer to what your unique gift is to share with the world!

You hold an incredible gift in this life. And when you learn how to use that gift, you will receive all the happiness, peace, and success that you crave. No one else can tell you what that gift is. Only you can discover it for yourself. And the only way to do that is through trial and error. Explore new pathways and find new goals. Be patient with yourself as you establish a strong bond with your soul, and here is where the truth of your gift will be revealed. Spend time nurturing love to your soul each day, and listen to the wisdom it speaks. Let your soul breathe through your being, let your energy align with your authentic truth.

You are about to embark upon a profound transformation of your life. All your greatest dreams and goals will be yours. Find faith in your ultimate success, and believe in it. Believe in yourself, believe in your soul, and believe in the divine power of the Universe, which is holding you so lovingly right now. Believe in your ancestors and spirit guides, your angels, and your loved ones. Believe in all of the good that surrounds you. Believe in the energy that is supporting you and providing you with this great change. You need to receive these blessings of change, even if it's not what you desire right now. You will survive this challenging moment in time. You will triumph and succeed. Because your soul believes you can handle this. You have great strength within you. You have unlimited power inside of you. And today is the day to tap into that power, harness that strength, and believe that you are divinely looked after by your Higher Self at all times, because you are. You truly are. You always are.

When You Need More Self-Care

I know it might be hard, but you need to start putting yourself first. No one is going to do it for you. And you won't gain anything from others stealing your time. You must prioritize your mental, physical, and spiritual well-being because, when you do, you will naturally become the best version of yourself. This, in turn, will enable you to be of greater help to others.

When someone is in need of healing, only a healed person can assist them. When someone wants to feel loved, only someone who truly loves themselves can guide another to feel that love. You have the power to heal, care for, and love others, but in order to do so, you need to fulfill those needs within yourself first. You are whole and complete on your own. The more you focus on caring for yourself, the easier it will be to share your love with another without depleting your own energy.

Your natural energy is radiant, brilliant, and blissful, but to stay in this state of pure lightness of being, you need to be aware of your energy levels as it fluctuates. Do you feel exhausted? Is your energy drained and lethargic? Do you need some soulful peace? Then your energy is asking to be cleansed, revitalized, and cared for. Spend some time today honoring your energy. Spend time today giving love back to yourself. What do you need to gift yourself? Ask your soul to guide you, and be open to the signs on how to follow through. The more we communicate and listen to the voices of our Higher Selves, the easier it will be to find the truth of what we need.

Once you learn what that process is, and what those practices are, you will notice how good you feel when doing them. And you will happily do them often because you will feel your energy radiating with eternal bliss. But the key to truly embodying those high vibrations is to practice your self-care routine *daily*. Move your energy, harness different vibrations, and cleanse your energy often. This is the pathway to finding the self-love and self-care healing that you need.

Too often we place our faith in others, waiting for them to show us the pathway forward. We hope that another may have the answers, or will make an effort to ensure we are looked after first. But you have all the answers that you need within you. You have all the power to find the truth of what you seek. The pieces of love that you need to fill yourself up with are already within you. The spaces of health and care that you desire are always around you. It's up to you to open your heart to listen, to walk, and to live with the care that you are craving. And then, once you do this, once you fill yourself up with all the love that you are seeking, you will be able to give all the love, all the laughter, all the light to those around you. Teach others how to respect your energy and time by respecting yourself first.

When You Need to Believe in Something

Know this. If ever you are faced with darkness, there is one thing you can always rely on. And there's one thing that will always get you through. I'm talking about faith. A belief in the higher good, in your greatest self, in the power of your soul. The faith that everything is happening for a reason. The faith that everything is going to work out just fine. Faith that your soul is within you, guiding you along your life path, directing you toward your destiny. Faith that whatever happens to you right now, is what is meant to happen because you have the strength to withstand any challenge.

Even if you are faced with the harshest circumstances, hold faith that you will get through this. Believe in your connection to the divine and your inner power of cosmic intelligence. Have faith that everything is going to be okay. And if you don't have faith, find it. Find that hope to get you through. Because this faith will be your strength to keep going no matter what. When we have faith in ourselves, and our life path, we are never let down. The road may be bumpy or a roller coaster at times, but we always end up where we are meant to. And we always end up better than where we started.

Find your faith by spending time connecting with your soul. Close your eyes, and feel the love from the unseen realms until you find it. Allow the energy of your soul to illuminate your presence, and let that loving light shine brightly in this darkness. The words of your soul will give you calm, peace, and clarity.

The energy of your soul will provide you with love, hope, and healing. Talk to your soul. Ask for answers. Ask for guidance. Ask for support. And be open to receiving the gifts it has to offer you.

When we hold faith, we are saying that we believe in ourselves. That we believe in our unique presence in this world and in our life path. When we have faith, we are taking our power back. We believe that everything will work out in our favor. When we have faith, we look at everything in our life as an integral tool for our own personal development journey. And we use that tool to self-improve, to be better, to live better. Even when faced with what seems to be impossible obstacles and challenges to overcome, we change our perspective on those experiences to view them as opportunities for transformation. And those opportunities support us in being the best version of ourselves that we can be, and in living the life we have always desired.

You are brilliant, resilient, and brave. You can handle anything that comes your way. You hold the ability to believe in yourself right at this moment. So choose it. Choose to believe in your power. Choose to believe that you are guided, supported, and loved by your Higher Self—always. Choose to believe in the power of faith, and let that faith shine brightly from your heart, sprinkling love and positive energy over anything and everything in your world.

When You Need a Break From People

Take a deep breath, my love, everything is going to be okay. I know they are hurting themselves by being so foolish. I know you know better, but it's not your path to take. It's their journey. It's their journey to fall down. It's theirs to stand up. It's theirs to learn how to transform and evolve. And although you think that by speaking your truth they will learn, they will heal, and they will change; they have not, and perhaps they don't want to right now. For they are who they are; therefore, you must learn to be okay. Accept them for who they are, and if you cannot find peace in this, make a conscious choice to walk away. Find the boundaries that support your growth, and hold them strong to keep your energies apart. Imagine protection, but send them love, and stay focused on your own inner journey.

Those feelings that arise within you and overpower your mind, hold great lessons for you too. For when we find irritation in another, it's important to look within to see where that irritation exists inside ourselves. What are they reflecting in your own life that you do not agree with? What emotions or actions are they embodying that are causing you so much pain? Do not ignore that irritation. For this is how stress will form in your body, this is how dis-ease will erupt if you don't address it. But to address it is not to act out onto them. Instead, make changes within yourself to react better, be kinder, more compassionate, more gentle, and more at peace. Keep building strength within yourself, my love, and keep moving your vibrations closer to that shining light inside your heart.

Allow your energy to move toward the vibrations that raise you up high, keep you lifted, and complement your life. Choose to find the peace, choose to share that peace with others, and always choose to live your life with love from your heart.

There is no need to worry. Their words and actions are not your responsibility. They will sort their life out with time. All you can do right now is lead by example. And acknowledge what your soul needs to feel safe. Give yourself space from others if your soul is calling for it. And focus on making a shift within your mind to gift yourself the peace you need. Turn to your meditations, and ask the cosmic world for strength. Ask your angels for guidance on how to proceed. Speak to your soul, and listen to its wisdom. You will be shown a pathway to find the answers you need. Allow the energy of irritation and anger to be heard, but find its reasons, find its wisdom, and then channel that energy into projects that support your personal growth for a better you. Find the joy within your life, find the soothing vibrations you seek. Keep your mind busy, and know that, with time, your heart will be at peace, just as theirs will too.

When You Need Self-Discipline

You know exactly what you need to do to achieve your goals. Your intuition has been telling you. Your spirit guides have been sending you clear signals. The whole Universe has been uniting to support you in following through with the changes that you crave. But you are holding yourself back. Even though you know how to walk the pathway forward. Why? It's because you lack the self-discipline to follow through, and procrastination has been your friend. But what are you waiting for? Only *you* can make the changes in your life to receive the success you crave. Only *you* can make the choices that will benefit your future. Only *you* can do it. No one else can. You've always known what is best for you. You know what's best for your life. Because your soul tells you this. And it has been telling you this for a while now. But you have been ignoring its calls.

Self-discipline doesn't need to be hard. You can find a way to make it fun. All it takes is a shift of perception and a commitment to a better self. And when we apply those two tools to our minds, we are determined to harness the power of our inner strength. The more you practice utilizing your inner strength, the more powerful you become.

But how do we find that self-discipline when we fear that we have none? Start by reminding yourself how you will feel when you achieve your goals. Remind yourself of the incredible success that is waiting for you. And define that success clearly. Think about what it will really mean to you when you are able to achieve it.

Envision yourself living your life with that success. Envision yourself feeling that euphoric high you crave; whether it be success business-wise, a healthy body, or time-managing your day to be stress-free. Look at where you need to change your life, and make a simple commitment to yourself. Find what areas require self-discipline, and make a plan. Ask for help from others if you need. Set yourself tiny, bite-sized goals with rewards, make yourself accountable, and then practice them consistently.

All it will take is dedication and persistence, both of which you hold already. But you have been ignoring the power of your divinity. Today you will no longer. Because you can do this! We all believe in you!

So today is the day that your life will change. Today you will commence your powerful self-discipline practice and follow through with it. Write down your goals. Make a list of what needs to be changed. Make a plan on how you will make those changes, and set yourself a time limit. And most importantly, make a commitment to yourself to follow through. Because you can. The only person who can do this is you. The only person getting in your way is you. You are the answer to all of your life's problems. You are the key to your future. You. It all starts with you.

When You Need to Keep Going After Failure

Failure. Too many of us are scared of this word. It's a fear that can overpower our rationality and stop us from moving forward. The fear of failure and what everyone would think of us is the sole reason half of us don't even try. And if we continue to think that we aren't good enough, then of course we won't succeed. But only you can choose to set the definition of what success means. And in the same realm, you choose what failure means. Make them work on your terms. Set mini-goals for success so you can tick them off. Make that first step of success achievable so that when you excel past it, the thought of failure will be far away. But even so, failure is never a bad thing. In failure, we find strength and answers. Through experimenting and taking risks, we are able to give meaning to life. Because hidden in our failures, we can find profound wisdom and growth. There is always something to be revealed with every change of direction.

The only people who fail are those who give up. So that's the only promise you need to make to yourself—to continue to persevere, to stay strong, to stay resilient. Keep your gaze focused straight ahead. Don't look at either side. Don't worry about what anyone else is doing, just focus on your own path. Focus on the brilliance that you hold. Focus on harnessing your talents and nurturing your ability to succeed. Focus on your inner power. Focus on your love and dedication. And whenever you feel tired, rest, don't give up. Take some time to rejuvenate your energy and then pick yourself back up and start over again. Keep your goals clear in your mind as you focus on achieving them.

Know that success takes time and hard work. Success is never quick and easy. It's a constant challenge. It's an ongoing conversation with the Universe, showing it how much you want it and what you will do for it. And it's about creating a plan to work alongside it. Keep that plan flexible, and be open to changing it. Know that, with time, your plan may change, but that it will grow with strength as you tick off your goals. You will achieve your goals in this life. You will succeed at everything you are dreaming of. Because it's your dream. It's your soul's vision. It's your life path.

There is no one on this Earth like you, and we need you in it. We're all cheering for you to succeed. Because when you succeed, we all succeed. We are all connected to the collective unconsciousness, and to live alongside your success brings great peace to the whole world. Your success reminds others of what they are capable of. And we need more people like that in the world. People who want to see each other rise up. People who want the best for everyone. Those people have a heart of gold, and they will be rewarded. That's you. You are chosen. You are incredible. And your life is going to be exactly that—a wondrous pathway of miracles and manifested dreams coming forth into fruition.

When You Need to Live in the Present Moment

Everything that lies before you, and everything that has already been, doesn't matter. All that matters is the energy you hold right now at this moment. The pain from your past has the ability to stain your vision. But it doesn't have to take control if you don't allow it to. You have the power to put the past to rest and to gift your mind the beauty of peace. All you need to do is align your focus with the present moment.

When we live in the present moment, there is no space for heartache. There is no anger, pain, or grief to be found. There is only peace waiting for you there. You can harness that peace for yourself. You can embody that peace wholeheartedly if you wish. You can allow that peace to completely overtake your energy with calm fluidity. To enter this peace is easy, but to stay there requires practice and dedication. Spiritual tools such as meditation and regular connection with Mother Nature will pave the pathway forward to harnessing this peace with longevity.

Be aware of your own energy, accept it, and then transform it into what you desire. Recognize that you have pain in your past, but let it be a piece of your story, not your whole story. It's just a chapter of what has been.

Recognize that it affected you, that it hurt you, and that it changed you. It has shaped who you are today, but it doesn't solely define you. It has influenced your perception of the world around you, but you can control whether to allow that influence to be positive or negative. You can rise up from this challenge with brilliance, and you can do this by facing it, by healing it, and by choosing to live with it in the present moment.

Today, simply let go of what has been, what could be, and what is. Take a deep breath and release your emotions, and align with the present moment. Let go of your fears, let go of your pain, and let go of any anxious thoughts by simply choosing to release and invite in beautiful positive vibrations that honor your soul right here, right now.

Because you deserve to live in peace. You deserve to live free of sorrow and grief. You deserve to live with whatever energy you crave. So what energy do you wish to hold today? Is it peaceful? Is it happy, loving, or joyful? Search for it around you. Discover it within you. And recognize it inside of you, as you live wholeheartedly in alignment with the present moment.

When You Need to Stop Feeling Lonely

"Is anyone out there?" you ask.
"Yes!" sing the voices of your angels.
"Yes!" cry the sounds of your ancestors.

They never left you. Not even for a second. They are watching over you, caring for you, and looking after you. They are giving you all the right lessons, and all the spiritual tools to help you step into the divinity of who you really are. Call out to them often, and feel their energy. The quieter you become, the louder their energy can be felt.

You have a whole spiritual army cheering you on. They are showering you with love, blessings, and guidance. They don't ever want you to feel alone. But they also know that, sometimes, feeling lonely is necessary for you to truly discover your gifts. They know that, sometimes, it's important to feel alone in this world so that you can harness the connection with your soul. Because once you reveal that unbreakable bond with your soul in the unseen realms, the voice of your intuition becomes loud and clear. And this voice of your intuition is the voice of your soul, and it is the voice that will carry you forward, that will bring you home, and remind you that you are never alone.

The more time you spend alone with your soul, the louder the wisdom of your life purpose becomes. You remember the true divinity of who you really are.

You will recall the power of your inner strength and the importance of your uniqueness. In this sacred space of alone time, you will harness the gift of what you bring to the world. In this alone time, you learn the truth about your unique presence in this world. So in this time of loneliness, turn your attention inward to feel the power of your soul speaking loudly to you. Close your eyes, take a deep breath, and listen to the guidance from your soul telling you how to spend this time to become a better version of yourself. Gift yourself love, gift yourself peace, gift yourself a moment to really learn who you are and what you desire. All of the answers to the questions that you hold will be revealed in this sacred space between you and your soul.

Can you feel the energy of your soul holding you tightly? Can you feel the energy of your angels by your side? Your ancestors, spirit guides, and angelic energy are all around you and embracing you with love and healing vibrations. Close your eyes, place your hand on your heart, and let your vibrations be soothed. Because you are never alone. Do you hear me? You are never alone.

When You Need to Remember How Incredible You Are

You. Beautiful, talented, inspiring you. You are so important to this world. You are crucial to the evolution of consciousness. Why? Because of who you are. Because of your divinity. Because of your pure and good nature. Your connection with all that surrounds you is necessary for the healing of the world. And because of this reason, you are praised, honored, and celebrated.

The world needs you in it. I need you in it. We all need you in it. Because your unique perception of how the world works is useful, compassionate, and graceful. There is so much goodness in your heart. There is so much more beauty in your life to be revealed, so much more wisdom and intelligence to be harnessed. You are only just beginning to truly embody and live your authenticity, and we're all excited to see how you evolve.

You are a child of the Universe, and you are learning the truth of what that means. You are learning how to mold and evolve through the vibrations of what it is that surrounds you. And so, you choose to surround yourself with goodness, and with beauty, and with abundance. And why not? You can create any life you wish to, so let's make it bountiful! Let's make it joyful, wondrous, and filled with high vibrations!

You have the power at your fingertips to create the changes that you seek. You can change your life in ways that support the illumination of your shining soul. So do it! Today, go forth with confidence toward your desires. Go forth with the support of the Universe sending you love. And step forward to live the life you crave. Because you are worthy of receiving all the incredible experiences and loving vibrations you deserve. You don't need to cower away anymore. You don't have to side with fear or limiting beliefs. You don't have to apologize for being the bright, shining star that you are. Because your divinity is what makes you unique. Because your gifts, your talents, and your love are needed today. Don't shy away. Don't hide the truth of who you really are. Don't be scared. Be you. Trust in your divine power. Live as yourself right now at this moment. Because you are so incredibly talented, loved, and cherished. More of us need to see the real you, more of us need to fall in love with your gifts. More of us need to see you here living your best life and sharing that life with others. That's what we want of you. That's what we want from you—to be yourself, to love yourself, and to believe in yourself. Because the moment you do, everyone else will be inspired to do it too. And from this space, anything is possible.

When You Need to Heal From Someone Who Hurt You

What they did to you was wrong. You weren't asking for it. You weren't being weak by not fighting harder. But it happened, and now you need to focus on your healing. But how do you heal something that has broken you so deeply inside? How do you forget something that is unforgettable? How do you rebuild the trust you once had?

You remind yourself of the strength you hold to overcome anything that comes your way. You remind yourself of the resilient nature you have acquired over many lifetimes. And you remind yourself that you are going to heal and move through this pain to live your greatest life.

But in order to heal anything, you need to first accept that it happened. Accept the truth of your experience, and be at peace with it. Allow any emotions to arise upon doing so, and simply observe them without any judgment. Any thoughts or feelings that we suppress will linger until they are felt and heard. Let your emotions have a voice. Scream, shout, or cry for as long as you need to until that energy is released. Expel your feelings from your body with actions, words, or movements. You must reveal the truth of their existence, and honor their message so that new vibrations can come into their place.

And when your energy of sadness, despair, and pain has been heard and released, you can breathe love into that wound. Every kind of love that exists channels that energy into your sacred temple. Call upon the endless love around you to soothe your sorrow. Seek nurturing vibrations from Mother Nature. Allow your emotions to be soothed through bathing in the water. Your pain is now a rite of passage, one that will shape your perception of reality forever. So call upon all the love that surrounds you: self-love, love for existence, love for others, love for the world and all the living creatures. Find the places, people, and things in your life that bring you happiness, that bless you with peace; and immerse your whole being into them. Let their energies comfort you. Let them breathe their vibrant existence into you. Let your body refuel, refill, and nurture your surroundings. Let yourself be you again. Take your time. Rest, and relax.

And that's it. That's the secret to healing yourself. Accept, release, renew, and revive. With every step forward, we acquire wisdom. With every new chapter, we become resilient. And with every step forward, we deepen the connection with our soul. This connection is the only thing constant in our life that will never change, that will never lead us astray.

When You Need to Be Forgiven for Hurting Someone

Okay, it happened. I know it's awful and you're so disappointed in yourself. But believe me when I tell you that everything is going to be okay. All you can do now is take accountability for your actions and seek forgiveness. Accept that it happened, and take the correct steps to right this wrong. You may feel like you have acted out of character, and perhaps this is true. For your shadow self may have taken over. Or maybe this was a build-up of a lot of pain. Perhaps you had been bottling up all of your sufferings for years and years, and it finally erupted. Whatever the reason, you caused another pain, and it was not your intention. You acted without thinking. It was an emotional overload that exploded into another. And, although it is wrong, we are human, and we all make mistakes.

Right now, all you can do is be self-aware of what happened, take responsibility for your actions, and ask for forgiveness. But before you do, understand why you acted the way that you did. And when you know why, share this understanding along with your apology. Apologize wholeheartedly to them, and then apologize to yourself. Make a promise to do better, to be better, and to learn from this mistake. Holding ourselves accountable is how we grow and evolve in our lives. Holding ourselves accountable is all that we can do during these unfortunate situations.

Recognizing where we have messed up is a strong form of self-awareness, and this quality is crucial for our evolution on the earthly plane.

Don't try to bypass this pain or ignore the repercussions. Face it, head on, and invite healing to take its place. For if you ignore or refuse to forgive, this pain can be carried over to future generations. So spend time really getting to know why you acted the way you did. Spend time alone self-reflecting so that you can grow from this mistake. Make sure you forgive yourself, and then do everything you can that feels aligned with who you are to right this wrong. When you finally move through this energy, you will transform with more compassion and resilience. You will heal, and they will heal. And you will ease this difficult period of your life through perseverance and personal development.

It's happened, so accept it, apologize, learn from it, and let it go. Our actions and words that come after self-reflection make us stronger. And most often, it's the most difficult experiences that bring us the most rewards. We learn invaluable tools for our life journey when this happens. So find the positive in this madness. Find the love, find the care, and find the healing vibrations that will soothe your soul as you navigate this difficult period of your life. Everything is going to be okay.

When You Need to Remind Yourself of How Far You've Come

Be gentle with yourself today. Take a deep breath, and remember all the good that exists in your world, because you created it. You created so many incredible things just by being yourself. There are so many miraculous elements in your life, and they are all there because of you. Everything wonderful that you have accomplished in your life exists because of you. It's because of your unique presence, your enthusiasm for understanding, and your desire for success. Your life is decorated with beautiful vibrations because of your willingness to never give up. Your life is blessed with fulfilling experiences because of your desire for change. It's because of your belief in the Universe. Remember your strengths, remember your power, and most importantly, remember how far you've come.

Everything that exists in your life, you once dreamed about. Whether you remember it or not, you did. You once thought about these possibilities, these opportunities, and therefore they manifested with brilliance. Everything in your life is there because you once wished for it, and after some time, they finally came true. Find those things in your life, and give gratitude to them. Remember when you once wanted them and what you did to achieve them. Write a list if you need to remind yourself. And write a list of all the things that you crave right now. And then watch as time passes and you gradually tick off each of your goals throughout your life.

Sometimes we may want something so badly, but the Universe has other plans. It doesn't mean that what you want isn't coming or that it's not a part of your destiny. It is. But, maybe you have a few life lessons to learn on the way before your manifestations can be delivered. Maybe there's something already waiting for you, but your focus is set elsewhere. Let go of what you think you should have, and accept, honor, and trust that where you are right now is exactly where you need to be. Hold onto faith that what you want is coming, and remind yourself that you are destined for greatness. And most importantly, give yourself confidence as you remember all the wonderful vibrations that you have brought into your life because of who you are.

You have persevered through difficult times. You have overcome huge challenges. You have triumphed in the face of darkness. And as a result, what happened? You became stronger. You became more compassionate to yourself. You became wiser. You gain something with each challenge that you overcome, and you have overcome so much. Don't forget about your wisdom. Don't forget about your resilience and inner strength. Don't forget about how far you've come.

When You Need to Let Go of Fear

You are wasting your beautiful energy by choosing to side with fear. You are holding yourself back from living as your truly beautiful self and restricting your ability to step into greatness. Fear exists, yes, but how you choose to handle that fear is still your choice. You can make a decision that empowers you or hinders your growth. What do you want to choose today? If you wish to stay small, for you are unsure of how to conquer it, just know that with time and determination, you will find the confidence you seek to overcome this fear. But when you finally let go of this fear and realize how easy it was, you may hold regret that you didn't do it sooner. But stay calm, it was your choice, and we must always stand by our choices.

If you are ready to face this fear and heal this trauma, then I have a sacred message for you today. It is to remind you that you are the creator of your life. You are the architect of your future. So you can, and you will, triumph and rise above this fear. How you wish to do this is up to you. You can find out the best pathway forward by confronting this fear and asking what it needs. What does this fear need from you today? Does it need more information? Are you fearful of what you do not know? Are you telling yourself a story about this fear? And is this story the truth? Or is it a fictional tale of what could be? If so, switch that mentality around, and find the most credible possibility that could be the reason why this fear exists. And then, confront it. Find reasons why it's not true, and lean closer to the side of love.

Take small steps as you confront your fears. Do whatever you feel is safe and authentic. There's no need to rush. There's no race to win. But if these fears are taking over the comfort of your daily life, then address them. Find out why they are there and how you can release them. Do what you can to tackle their existence. Find your spiritual tools to support your growth. Find the spiritual resources that encourage you to live the life that you deserve. You do not deserve to live in fear. You deserve to shine brightly and live a life filled with high vibrations and miraculous adventures.

Everything that you wish for is merely at your fingertips. Don't let these negative thoughts or fears hold you back from receiving your destiny. Let them go. Step closer to the brave and courageous you. The real you. Step forward and embrace the divine light that beats courageously within you, and let it take charge. Feel the love of your soul guiding you on your pathway forward, and know that you are divinely guided, supported, and protected by the Universe at all times.

When You Need to Be Held

I feel your pain. I know what you need. You need someone to hold you and tell you everything is going to be okay. But there is no one around you. There is only yourself. There is only your soul, and your soul is tired. So what do you do? Where do you go? You go out into Mother Nature, and let her hold you. Lie down in her sweet embrace. Let her loving vibrations soothe your soul. Let her healing energy bring you peace. Let her angelic spirit save you. She wants to help. She is never too busy to help. It is never the wrong time for her to help. All you need to do is ask.

You are always surrounded by the bountiful blessings of Mother Nature. Her energy vibrates with only the highest frequencies, and these vibrations have the power to take away your pain. Mother Nature's love will embrace you at your weakest moments, at your lowest self, and she will fill your soul up with tender loving care. She will provide you with both softness and strength. She reminds you to keep going. Her energy will help you see things clearly. Her energy protects you, heals you, and nurtures you. Seek her guidance, and ask for her help. Feed her your pain, your worries, your stress, and your hurt. And let her take those emotions and transform them into greatness. And in return, she will give you her blessings, her love, and her happiness.

You deserve to live a life full of abundance, but you may have difficulty creating this space on your own. And no one is expecting you to. That's what Mother Nature is there for. She is there to support you, help you, and nourish you. She is there to soothe your vibrations with peace and love. She is the mother of creation who will nurture your soul with the magical energy of Source Creation. She brings you home, to where you came from, to where you belong, and holds you tightly, reminding you of all that exists within you. She is created from the same cosmic intelligence that created you, and together, you re-energize each other. She will always hold you, she will always love you. She will always be there waiting for you, ready to bring you back home. All you need to do is ask.

So today go and visit her. Let the soft illumination of sunlight awaken your spirit. Breathe in the sweet perfume of fresh air, and let your energy be cleansed and invigorated. Let your bare feet touch the Earth and ground your soul into your body as you heed the ancient wisdom of her blessings. Listen to the chorus of nature's sounds as you allow your energy to absorb the bountiful vibrations that surround you. Let your body melt into her sweet embrace. Let her love fill up your soul, and let her hold you tightly. Open yourself to receive her blessings. Let her love bring you home.

When You Need Life to Flow Differently

I know life has been hard right now, and that there's no other reason for it than "just because." And that not knowing why can sometimes be more frustrating than the challenge itself. But today I want you to trust that everything is going to work out. Today I want you to understand that everything is as it should be.

Because not accepting what is will only keep you in pain. And resisting how your life wants to flow, will stop your ability to grow. You need to accept your life, no matter how difficult it is, and then you will be in a place of strength, so that you can make the changes that you seek. You need to take back your power, and the best way to do that is to be at peace with what is happening.

Life will flow with ease the moment you accept the way your life is now, right at this moment. Because holding tightly to wishing things could be different is only hurting yourself. Holding firmly to expectations of how your life should be is only causing you pain. It isn't serving you any favors. The longer you resist what is, the longer this pain will engrave into your mind. The sooner you let go and accept your life, the sooner you will be at peace. Because your life path is predestined to deliver the most miraculous, incredible, and blissful experiences that you could only dream to be possible. And even if you don't believe it right now, you are living them!

So today don't think that you know best. Don't assume that life should be a certain way. Instead, accept it, love it, give thanks for it, and surrender the need to control it. Silence your mind, and listen to the voice of your soul calling out to you. Believe in your inner power because you have the strength to persevere in these times of darkness. You have the confidence and resilience to overcome any challenges laid out before you. All you need to do is believe in yourself. Believe in your divine presence in this world. Believe that even when nothing feels like it's right; know that it's actually working out in your favor. Because it always is. People leave and relationships fall apart so that new beginnings can ignite, and these kinds of unexpected changes in our lives can bring forth incredible rewards.

Even in times of great despair, there's an invitation for transformation laid out before you. And this invitation is going to open the doorway to your greatest self. It's going to remove all of those layers of your insecurities and fears and open you up to greatness. But to get to this place, you need to allow your energy to become moldable. You need to let go of how you think your life should be, and accept what's going on in your life right now. Because the moment you do will be the moment you will feel at ease. And when you feel at peace, your soul speaks clearly, you live life deeply, and everything finally feels like it's going to be all right.

When You Need to Feel Healthy

The mind is an incredibly powerful thing. It thinks that it's in charge of your actions and thoughts, yet, in truth, you actually have complete control over it. But taking control of your mind takes practice. And living out this truth takes discipline. And to do so requires one thing—for your soul to speak clearly and loudly to you. And most importantly, for you to listen to that radiant soul of yours.

Right now, your soul is telling you that your health is of the utmost priority. You are being told that you need to make big changes in your life to nurture love back into your body. Your body is crying for attention. It is screaming for you to listen. It is telling you that it needs tender loving care and to be taken care of. But you've been busy. You've been moving and shaking so fast that you have been neglecting its beauty. But you can't keep running away from what your body needs any longer. For this body that you carry is your divine temple. It is a sacred space that is hosting your soul. Your body deserves to be honored. Your soul chose your body, your mind, and your life here on Earth. Don't disrespect its wishes because you aren't listening to what it needs.

If you learn how to listen to what your body needs, you will make your health a priority. And when you prioritize this regularly, you will be on the right path to preventing serious health problems and diseases in the future. And if you nurture your health properly, before you're forced to, it may not have to be your greatest life lesson to master.

You can heal your body with the right foods, environment, and physical care; if you would just give yourself a chance. You have the inner power to be whoever you want to be, and that doesn't stop at your thoughts and actions, it follows through to your lifestyle and body. What kind of health do you want? What type of body do you wish to live in? And what can you do to achieve those dreams? What changes in your life can you make today, tomorrow, and in the future? And how can you be sure that you stick to it? Reveal your weaknesses to find your solutions. Reveal your desires for a healthy body, and create a healthy mind to match the vibrations that you seek. And once you know what that is, practice it consistently until you achieve the goals that you desire.

Health is something attainable to you today, right here, at this moment. All it requires is the combination of education and the diligent application and repetition of healthy habits. It requires a healthy mindset with the mental clarity to achieve your goals. You have the strength to embody the health that you desire and crave, all you need to do is believe in yourself. We all believe in you. Now we need you to believe in yourself too.

When You Need to Believe in Yourself Because No One Else Is

I feel you. I've been there before. I know what it feels like to be the only one cheering you on. And it can be such a lonely road to go down. You have a great deal of ambition within you, driving you forward and telling you that this is the pathway, but you look around, and there is no one there to agree with you or even support you. There is only yourself following this road to what you dream to be a victorious success. When there's no one else supporting your goals, how do you keep going? You connect with your soul. You speak to the Universe. You call upon your spirit guides for assistance. You ask your soul, "Is this my life path? Should I keep following my passions and dreams?" And if the answer is yes, then you keep going! Because if you keep going and persevere, no matter what happens, you will succeed because this is your destiny.

And if you get stuck along the way, if you find yourself falling too many times, you check in with your soul, and you realign once more. You call out to your spirit guides. You say to them, "I am wavering from my path, tell me what to do." And then sit with yourself in silence and listen to the wisdom. Is your soul telling you that this is your destiny? Is your soul confirming that this is your ultimate craving? Is your soul telling you that this is the life you are destined to live? And if it is, you keep going.

You will always face difficulties along the path that is meant for you. Because this is a chief component of your soul contract. If the path to your ultimate success was easy, it wouldn't feel so rewarding when you finally *do* make it. Your life journey was always meant to be filled with complex challenges to overcome, a surplus of emotions to move through, and important decisions to steer your destiny forward. You have the power to make these choices with confidence, but to do so requires an unshakable bond with your intuition. Because it will be the voice of your soul guiding you forward during times of despair.

If you are feeling unloved and unmotivated, this is a drastic calling to reconnect with the spirit world. This is a sign to speak to your guides, to nurture love within your soul, and to reconnect with what lights a spark inside your being. You are lost for only a mere moment, my darling. Do not fear, do not fret. For the divine love and light that you seek is within you. I believe in you. We all do. The whole Universe, your angels, your spirit guides, and most of all, your soul, is driving you forward. We are all cheering for you, supporting you, and sending you love in the unseen realms. Connect with us here, and we will feed you all the love and care that you need today. Place your hands on your heart, close your eyes, and sit in silence, allowing the voices of nurturing vibrations to enter through and bring you peace.

When You Need to Let Go of the Past

Okay, it happened. Yes, it's sad. Yes, it's heartbreaking. And perhaps you're angry at the Universe for allowing such a tragic episode of your life to play out. But before you fall down into a sorrowful cry of victimizing blame, let's acknowledge that these experiences have the ability to make you grow stronger.

Every single challenge that you encounter is testing your patience, your connection with your soul, and your faith in the Universe. It is asking you to choose; choose between whether you are abandoned in this world, destined to find failure and loss, or whether you are divinely guided, destined to live a life filled with high vibrations and ultimate success. Let me tell you today, and please listen carefully—you are always divinely guided, cared for, and looked after by the Universe. You are never alone. And what has happened in your life has happened for a reason. Yes, sometimes that can be an awful thought because what happened to you may be so painful and hurtful that you can't possibly imagine how to see the light. But hold faith that, with time, you will. There is profound wisdom waiting to be embraced in your aura. This wisdom has always been a part of you, and when you finally acknowledge it, you will be able to see things more clearly than before. Finding the reason why is not the purpose of this pain. Because the answers will come to you when the time is right. Instead, focus your attention on how to heal, how to let go, and how to move forward. Because this is all you need right now. And this is what you can control.

The experiences that we face in life can throw our emotions down into the depths of survival. But you have the power within you to transform into greatness. And these challenges are exactly what you need in order for your soul to evolve. Your soul asked for these lessons before it entered the earthly plane. It wanted to feel these emotions and learn how to overcome such turmoil. And so, for this reason, there is absolutely nothing that you can't handle. Your soul wanted these challenges so that your energy could transform into something greater. Because with every challenge that you overcome, you evolve with wisdom. When we heal, we strengthen the connection with our soul, we hear the voice of our intuition louder, and we surrender more freely to the magical workings of the Universe.

So today let yourself feel the pain from the past, but do not let it overtake your happiness. Do not let it sink so deeply into your mind that you cannot move forward. Be kind to yourself. Let your emotions be released gently with love. Accept them, feel them, and then let the experience go. Use your breath to assist you deeply, use Mother Nature to hold you tightly. And release that painful experience from your memory. Trust that it was needed to enable you to grow stronger. Trust that these lessons are important for your evolution in your life. And most importantly, have faith that you are always looked after and guided with love from the Universe.

When You Need to Heal From the Passing of a Loved One

I'm so sorry for your loss. I'm thinking of you and your loved ones. And I'm sending you healing prayers filled with so much love and lightness. I know your heart may be breaking right now. I know that you may be confused with grief as to how life could be so cruel. Or maybe you are searching for a pathway to move forward. Remind yourself that it's okay to stand still for a while. Honor this space as you remember who they were. Breathe their love and feel their energy. Remember the beautiful memories that you shared. Remember the positive light of their vibration. Remember the way they saw the world and the way that they made you feel.

Think about all the love that you shared together. All the tears of joy, all the emotions, and all the experiences that they ignited within you. They were as important in your life as you were in theirs. Hold peace in knowing that. They haven't gone far, it's only their energy that has moved to another place. It's their energy that has passed over. But you will meet them again one day. Until then, know that they will never leave you. Their angelic soul is watching over you now, protecting you, and sending you love.

Let the love that you feel for them bring their energy to you as often as you need. Let the words that you speak about them keep their energy alive. Let the way they made you feel be remembered on the days you miss them. And send them love as you celebrate the time you shared.

Hold comfort in knowing that they are in another place now, and that, one day, you will be reunited again. In another life. At another time.

Until that day happens, they will visit you in your dreams. They will send you messages through strangers and animals. For they are now an angel watching over your life, guiding you along your pathway, protecting you, and caring for you. They will always be sending you love and blessings. Be open to heed those blessings. Their voice may be quiet, but it will be powerful. And they will speak to you whenever you call for them.

Be gentle with yourself as you heal the grief in your heart. Connect with nature to nurture love back into your life. Find the simple joys around you that bring you pleasure and embody them fully to receive their peaceful vibrations. Take as much time as you need to honor their light. And speak to them often, out loud or through your soul. They will hear you. They will feel you. They will always, always be with you.

When You need to Find More Joy and Happiness

There is pain in your heart, I know. There is sadness in your gaze, I can feel it. But it doesn't have to be this way. You have the power to see things differently. You have the ability to love your life again. It just takes time. It may require healing. But you will feel yourself again, you will be the bright shining light that you always have been. You will soon see all the wonderful miracles that reside around you. But until that illuminating revelation comes, seek the small things that bring you joy.

Your whole world is filled with an abundance of both high and low vibrations. There are moments of pleasure and joy at your fingertips, waiting to be harnessed. Don't believe me? Get outside and visit Mother Nature! When was the last time you connected with her—truly? When was the last time you walked and marveled at her beauty? She heals you. She saves you. She nurtures your soul and calms your energy. She is your answer to reminding yourself of all the beauty still left in the world.

Mother Nature holds a gift for you to take today. Go and visit her, connect with her, and let her energy soothe your soul. Let your energy absorb her beauty as she invites you to align with the present moment. Listen to the birds sing, hear the soft rustle of wind through the leaves as you connect with the animals, and smell beautiful flowers to bring you joy. Feel the energy of her ancient trees, and look up into their branches, recognizing the wisdom that lies before you. Walk barefoot amongst the dirt, and feel the grounding energy of the Earth that supports you. Seek sunrises and sunsets, swim in freshwater, babbling brooks, or in the rhythmic waves of the ocean. Climb hills and mountains to discover new horizons that bring your eyes pleasure. Feel the rejuvenating breath of fresh air on your skin, and inhale its crisp energy. This will refresh and revitalize you. The abundance of natural resources will rebirth you.

You are standing still for a moment of time, needing a change in your environment. Seek out those changes yourself. Find them within, and search for them around you. Finding love and happiness in the small things will bring you back home to the magic of Source Creation. Finding the little pleasures in life will remind you that all is well. The smell of sweet jasmine flowers, the taste of fresh tomatoes, and the feeling of saltwater kisses on your skin. Nurture your mind, body, and soul with the plentiful gifts of Mother Nature. And then look to your soul and continue to feed it loving vibrations. What do you really want? What do you really need? Listen to your cravings, because it is your destiny. Whatever you desire today is where you need to go. And wherever you go, there is beauty to be found.

When You Need a Sign

There are so many wonderful blessings already in your life right now. You are surrounded by Mother Nature to heal, fresh water to cleanse, and at any moment of any day, you can relax with a peaceful meditation to connect with the spirit world and gain insight into your life. You have the power to choose your lifestyle, your friends, your career, and your safe space. You have an abundance of options around you at all times. And you have the ability to change those options if you wish.

But sometimes you don't always feel confident about your choices, and perhaps you find yourself not moving forward because you are waiting for a sign to tell you how. But it's time for you to stop waiting. Because standing still in your life, waiting for change to happen, doesn't serve any purpose. Your desire to search for a sign, is a sign in itself, telling you that you are craving change. And, therefore, this searching for an indication of the pathway you want is your prompt to do something.

You know the answers to every question you could ever ask. Your soul has all of this information in the spirit realm. Your job is to connect with your soul and listen to the guidance on how to move forward. When we ask for signs from the spiritual realm, we usually have a desired outcome in mind because our intuition is telling us the answers. But perhaps you have difficulty believing it because you are holding fear around the solution. So next time you ask for a sign, ask your soul to guide you forward, and trust the message from your inner voice.

Signs from the spirit realm and from your spirit guides often come to us when we least expect them. When we aren't searching or waiting, that's when they come. And they come in so many forms. Being open to the signs around you is key. Any wildlife that brings your attention and makes you think of something specific can be a sign. A stranger who tells you wisdom without you requesting it can be a sign. There are so many different ways for messages to come through to you. And often in life, they come when you aren't looking for them.

So today, if you are waiting for a sign, sit in silence with your soul and ask for guidance. If you cannot find the answers, tell your spirit guides you will go outside, and then go for a walk. Look around as you do, and let the answers come through to you. When we connect with Mother Nature, we are more receptive to the spirit realm, and we are able to feel things clearly. Trust and believe in your own divinity. Be at peace with your choices by listening to your intuition and staying aligned with the voice of your soul. And let your soul tell you the sign that you need to hear today.

When You Need Freedom

There is freedom within you. There is peace inside of you waiting to be harnessed. You hold the key to entering this space of nirvana. But you are keeping the door closed because you are scared or unsure of how to live in your authentic truth. You are searching for freedom in your *reality* when in truth, it exists in your *mentality*.

Freedom is a state of mind that we create through our perception of ourselves and the world around us. We can enter this space by choosing to live authentically in alignment with our true needs and desires. But to live in this truth, we need to see past the societal constraints and limitations placed in the reality around us. We need to heal from the trauma we have endured, the conditioning that has been inflicted upon us, and the social expectations and norms that have been unwillingly placed upon us. Through self-awareness and self-reflection, we can recognize that these constraints exist from the outside forces and are not a direct result of our internal doing. We can heal and align with the truth of our soul by cultivating self-acceptance and self-compassion. Spend time understanding your beliefs and actions to clearly define what it means to live as your authentic self. Once you have clarity over what this freedom means to you and how you can achieve this, speak your boundaries clearly, and protect your truth.

Choose to break through the mental barriers of resistance. Confront and dismantle anything that is holding you back from pursuing your passions and goals.

Recognize any areas of your life that are hindering your personal growth, and transform them to support the infinite opportunities that surround you. Embrace your inherent power, and engage in activities that promote self-liberation through a change of perception of yourself and the world around you. Find your inner peace through spiritual practices, accept yourself and your life in this moment to shift your perception to a place of power. For from this space, you can make changes that support your greater good and align with your authentic truth, which will provide you with your ultimate freedom. Take time to embody and understand your beliefs and desires in life, no matter what the world tells you. Find the peace and beauty in your decisions, and stand by them. Follow your truth, and you will find the freedom that you seek.

No matter what difficulties you face today, choose to find that sense of liberation within by connecting with your soul and reminding yourself of your power. Choose to find strength in your outlook on life, and choose to find peace through your actions and words despite any limitations from external factors. You always hold the power to choose your thoughts, your attitudes, and your beliefs. So choose to align with your truth as you seek to reveal and nurture the freedom within.

When You Need to Find Calm Amidst the Chaos

Deep breaths, my sweet child. Slow breaths, my darling. You have the power to calm yourself. You have the ability to soothe your vibrations by simply choosing to. Acceptance of self. Acceptance of love. Acceptance of peace. It is all around you. Tune into those vibrations. Tune into that energy.

You are calm. You have peace. You are supported.

You have the power to calm yourself using just your breath and intention. If you want to be aligned with calming vibrations, simply ask, and you will receive. Simply request, and follow your natural instinct to resonate in this space.

I am calm. I am peace. I am tranquil.

I slow my breath down into an elongated trance-like place. And with every breath in and every breath out, I am nurturing that loving energy into my heart. I allow my vibrations to soften into the air around me. I allow my energy to soothe itself using the Earth beneath me.

I am calm. I am at peace. I am supported by the love of the Universe.

I am completely in alignment with the energy around me. And with every breath in and every breath out, I relax even more. I feel my soul expanding amidst the magic of the Universe, receiving love, nurturing vibrations, and healing energy.

I am calm. I am at peace. I am supported.

I am aligned with the tranquil vibrations of the Universe around me. I am relaxed and in love with my own vibrational frequency. I am blissful at this moment. I am floating amidst the sacred space of timeless absence. I am soft yet resilient. I am strong but choose to be transparent. I am calm and free.

I am calm. I am at peace. I am living in alignment with my soul's destiny.

I breathe with ease. For the wisdom of my power has presented itself to me. I remember where I come from. I remember my truth. I remember my limitless strength. I have the resilience to handle anything that comes my way. I have combated much worse many lifetimes before. This challenge is merely a moment in my life that I will overcome. I simply turn to my soul, to the Universe, to Source Creation, and feel their blessings amplify within me once more.

When You Need Clarity Over Your Life

Everything that you find challenging in your life has the ability to change you. It has the power to create an entirely new you. One that is more aligned with the person you have always wanted to become. But sometimes we find it easier to hide than to confront our demons. Often, we would rather choose small comforts than feel uneasy. But what we fail to recognize is that this challenge has been put onto our path for a reason. And that reason is to transform you into the version of yourself you have always been craving.

But you never thought that becoming your greatest self would take hard work. You thought that life would just flow and things would go your way. You didn't know that to evolve into a wise warrior, you would need to endure endless battles. But this was always a part of your soul contract, and this is the experience your soul has been asking for. You are here to evolve and explore the depth of emotions that you have never known to exist before.

For when you rested so peacefully in the spirit world, in the realm of unconsciousness, immersed with all the wisdom, all the love, all the oneness with the Universe, you didn't know such feelings could be felt. You didn't know that these emotions could exist. All you knew was that facing challenges, both succeeding and failing, would enable your soul to evolve. And this is what you desired—your energy to expand.

So when you were offered to come down into the earthly plane you said: "Yes! I will take the bad with the good! I will feel the weight of sadness, grief, and despair if it means I can know what it feels to give love and receive it, to feel joy, laughter, and pleasure."

You wanted change. You wanted growth. You wanted wisdom. And now, you have all of these invitations for transformation at your fingertips, so will you cower away? Or will you step into the role that you had preconceived before existence? With each difficulty you face, you grow more resilient. You become lighter in your mind and wiser in your heart, with a deep sense of knowing that all is a part of the great master plan.

Your intuition is guiding you forward. It's lifting your feet to keep you walking. You are stopping here because you choose to. You are stopping here because you are scared. You are scared to learn what is lying on the other side of fear. You are scared to find yourself, to be yourself, to live as yourself—as your greatest self. Keep walking forward, my love. For it is there that you will find yourself. Open yourself to change and explore the life laid out before you. Analyze your intentions, values, and beliefs; and if they align with your goals, then this is where you need to be. And if not, then you change, and you make changes that suit the ultimate version of yourself. Take a deep breath, my love, keep journeying forward, and you will see things clearly once more, and you will be so very grateful that you never gave up.

When You need to Go to Sleep After a Difficult Day

I know today was difficult. I know all you wanted to do was run away and hide, but just know that tomorrow holds hope for the future. Tonight, rest your soul in a sweet cloud of dreams, as you journey to the spirit world, and let the healing vibrations of the Universe soothe you.

You can stay in this heavenly bliss for as long as you need. For there is so much love to be given to you there. Sleep soundly upon the floral scents of sweet perfume, as you travel to the unseen realms with your vibrant soul. Here you will meet with the spirits who have been guiding you, and here you will heed the wisdom from your ancestors' journeys. This is the wisdom to be found. . . .

"Go deeper," they say, as they whisper from above, from below, and within.
"Go deeper," they hum, as they breathe love with their prayers and sprinkle healing light upon your body.
"Go deeper," they cry, as they beat on their drums, cocooning your heart with peaceful vibrations, telling you to carry on.

And you awake with the knowledge of what is, what has been, and what could be. And you finally feel grateful for enduring the hardships. For you have grown stronger, you have received wisdom, and your perception of the world has changed forever.

So go to sleep, my darling. Rest that beautiful body upon the ground, and allow the Earth to soothe your energy. Let your soul travel into the unseen realms and connect with the energy that is waiting for you there. Let go of all your fears, all your sorrows, and your pain. Release all of that stuck energy you have been holding onto. Use your breath to sink deeper into relaxation. There is no space for you to hold onto this energy anymore. You are going to be filled up with new vibrations. With deep, heart-nurturing care. That is what you deserve, and that is what is coming to you. So let go, relax, and go to sleep. Know that everything will be better when you wake up tomorrow.

Sleeping Prayer

I call upon the energy around me. Bless me in my space, and send me sweet dreams so that I may heal my burdens from today. Give me the wisdom to my questions, the patience, and the understanding to be content with acceptance. And protect me while I sleep, guide me with complete safety so that I may rejuvenate my energy and rest my soul, and send me love.

Today

I welcome light into my aura.
I open myself to receive the blessings
from the Universe around me.
I gift myself grace and patience,
telling myself that all is as it should be.
And I go about my day,
smiling with love in my soul
and kindness in my heart,
knowing that everything is going to be okay.

About the Author

Phoebe Garnsworthy writes books that speak to your soul. She travels between the worlds of the seen and unseen, gathering ancient wisdom and angelic energy.
Her writings reflect a dance with the mystical and wonderful, an intoxicating love potion to devour in a world that overflows with forgotten love and enchantment.
The intention of her writing is to encourage conscious living and unconditional love.

www.PhoebeGarnsworthy.com

Other Books by Phoebe Garnsworthy

Daily Rituals: Would you like to attract more abundance? More love, more happiness, and more peace? It is available to you right now if you believe it to be true. Everything in existence is vibrating energy. Whatever you want can be yours - if you learn how to emit that vibrational frequency. And from this place, energy will magnetize toward you, naturally connecting like vibrations together. This enables you to attract what it is you wish to seek.

Align with Soul: In every challenge, we are handed an opportunity to evolve into a better version of ourselves. We are given a choice – either to keep repeating the same mistakes or to accept the invitation graciously and realize that we have the power within to be our own savior. We can learn how to heal and navigate a fulfilling life path by aligning with our soul to activate the wisdom of the universal love that surrounds us. Align with Soul will provide you with the spiritual philosophy, tools, and techniques to inspire your journey of personal development toward enlightenment.

Sacred Space Rituals: This book was created by calling upon ancient spiritual philosophy from around the world. It primarily uses the principles of creative visualization while harnessing the abundance of universal energies that surround you. The purpose of these rituals is to assist you in your journey of personal development and spiritual transformation.

I Affirm My Power: This book is the perfect combination of affirmations, daily rituals, spiritual practices, journal prompts, and meditations. Through the power of self-love and self-care, let Phoebe guide you to reveal the divine light within and to honor your soul.

Define Me Divine Me: A Poetic Display of Affection: Define Me Divine Me is an exploration of raw truth that provokes our deepest emotions so that we may honor both the light and the dark within us. Together, we allow the words of enlightened wisdom and painful beginnings to wash through us, as we stand back up and claim what is rightfully ours.

and still, the Lotus Flower Blooms: This spiritual poetry book explores the hardships we face throughout our lives and inspires you to search within to find the tools you need to survive. Like the lotus flower that grows through mud yet rises every day to greet the sunshine without a slither of darkness upon its petals, you will too, move through your life with grace, resilience, and beauty.

Lost Nowhere + Lost Now Here Series: The Lost Nowhere Book Series explores spiritual witchcraft in a fictional environment. While following the eclectic imagination of a girl called Lily, the reader is taken to another universe, a magical world called Sa Neo. In this enchanted world, you will meet powerful witches, shamans, healers, queens, kings, and mermaids. You will heed their spiritual wisdom while having all of your senses heightened, as you explore a world of beauty, magic, and miracles.

www.ingramcontent.com/pod-product-compliance
Lightning Source LLC
Chambersburg PA
CBHW070435010526
44118CB00014B/2056